I0488065

Miami @ Play 2018

© 2019 by Lindsay D. Grace, Lien B. Tran, and Clay Ewing

All rights reserved. This book or any portion thereof may not be reproduced or used in any manner whatsoever without the express written permission of the publisher except for the use of brief quotations in a book review or scholarly journal.

First Printing: August 2019
ISBN: 978-0-359-85219-2

New Experience Research and Design Lab (NERDLab)
University of Miami
School of Communication
5100 Brunson Drive, Coral Gables, FL 33146

http://www.MiamiPlay.com

CONTENTS

Acknowledgements

The organizers of the inaugural Miami @ Play exhibition would like to acknowledge the support provided by FilmGate Miami staff, in particular Diliana Alexander, Dom Narvaez, and Liz Pasillas.

The event was supported by generous funding provided by the John S. and James L. Knight Foundation. Equipment and technical support were provided by the University of Miami's School of Communication.

The team would also like to acknowledge University of Miami M.F.A. in Interactive Media students Laura Miller for assisting with this book's design and Manouj Govindaraju, Xihan Zu, and Zhuang Qian for providing technical assistance during the exhibition run.

Introduction

Miami @ Play is a curated collection of art and design work that seeks to demonstrate a range of playful experiences. This book provides a summary of the work presented at the first exhibition in late 2018. The curators provided an international call for artists submissions of both completed and proposed work with the following simple prompt:

> Whether toy, video game, board game, or big game, we aim to showcase how games can move us to joy, tears, critical reflection, and social impact. We seek work that exemplifies the diversity of play, its potentials, and the unique ways that games can build community, transcend language, and serve as an artistic medium.

Of the many submissions, the selected work, which is archived in this catalog of the exhibition, represents a truly original collection. The work touches on the character of play, both digital and analog. The curators aimed to offer perspective not only on the whimsical qualities of play, but also on the ways in which play inspires thought, reflection, new perspective, and meaning. While the recent history of games literature has produced specific terms like newsgame, social impact games, art games, and more, the aim of the exhibit was to not only recognize these forms but also provide an experience that acknowledges their overlap.

While the creators of such work may have specific aims, the work itself is often unified by a fundamental experience. That experience is play. Play is most easily understood as a carefree state that exists in the 'ordinary' world. While many assume that play is the opposite of work, many scholars and the oft cited play scholar Brian Sutton Smith acknowledge that the opposite of play is not work. Sutton-Smith writes in his 1997 treatise on play that play is "the willful belief in acting out one's own capacity for the future" (Ambiguity of Play, p. 198). What then does it mean to fail to play? If one fails to play with an idea, they fail to think critically about it. If one fails to play with ideas, they fail to think about the future. In this way play is not the ridicule or whimsy that is casually assigned to play; instead, it is respect and homage. To play with something is to acknowledge it and deem it worthy of such interactions. Thus, in this context, failing to play with someone is an assault and failing to play with something is a snub.

This need for interaction is evident in the design of playful experiences. Toys that are not played with are mere objects or artifacts reminiscent of play. Once played with, any object can be converted to a toy (a.k.a. a play object), elevating it to the honor and privilege of play.

Play requires interaction, which is why the curators believe in exhibiting such playful work. While the tradition of art exhibition oscillates between encouraging and prohibiting visitors to touch, it is perhaps the most appropriate way to understand playful work.

However, one of the great tragedies of modern, creative exhibitions of game work is a failure to archive the work. As websites archiving work fall prey to technical atrophy, the videos become harder to view at new resolutions and the work itself becomes harder to experience - in contrast with the durable, easily archived qualities of a print book.

Hence, this collection is offered as a way to understand work which 10 or 20 years from now may be inaccessible. Instead of relying on second hand reports, this collection reports the creators' work in their own words. Each of the selected artists for this first Miami @ Play was allowed a limited word count to describe their work and its relationship to the exhibition's theme. The result is a plethora of voices articulating what their work aims to do at the intersection of play and with various artistic intentions. There are some artists who look to expose current news topics in ways that are more meaningful to players. Others look to aid in the understanding of history, the novelty of a technical experience, or that imbue the Dada intersection of meaning and whimsy.

Likewise, each experience in the collection is varied in its aesthetics. Some are very traditional implementations while others are novel. From retrofitting game hardware to providing metaphors for the fragile equilibrium of life's responsibilities, the work has depth both in concept and experience.

Please enjoy this archival record of Miami @ Play 2018.

References:
Sutton-Smith, Brian. *The ambiguity of play*. Harvard University Press, 2009.

GRACE | TRAN | EWING

EXHIBITION

The Miami @ Play 2018 exhibition was held at 155 South Miami Avenue in Downtown Miami.

It was open to the public and co-located with the 2018 FilmGate Interactive Festival's Extended Reality (XR) Portal.

EXHIBITION

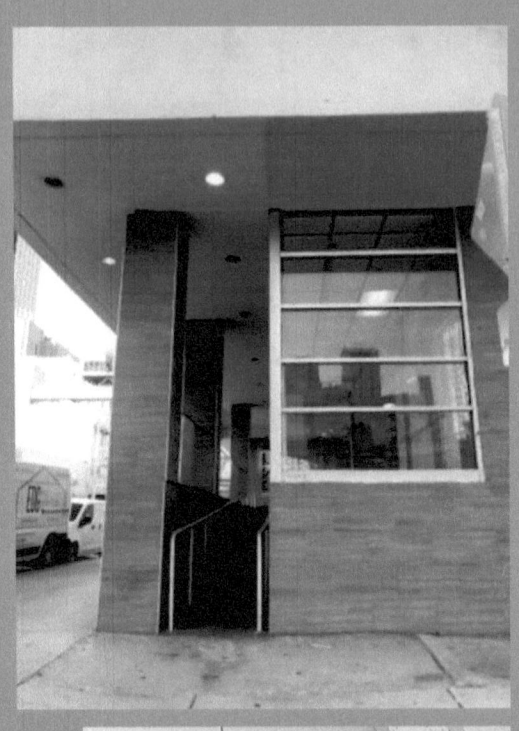

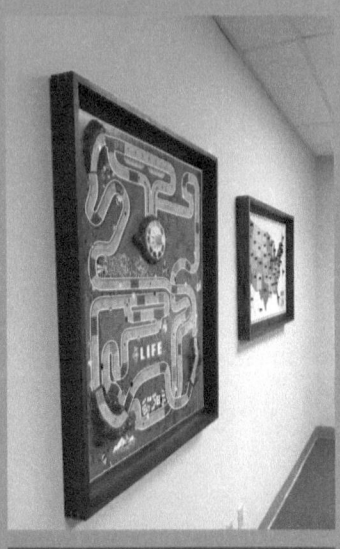

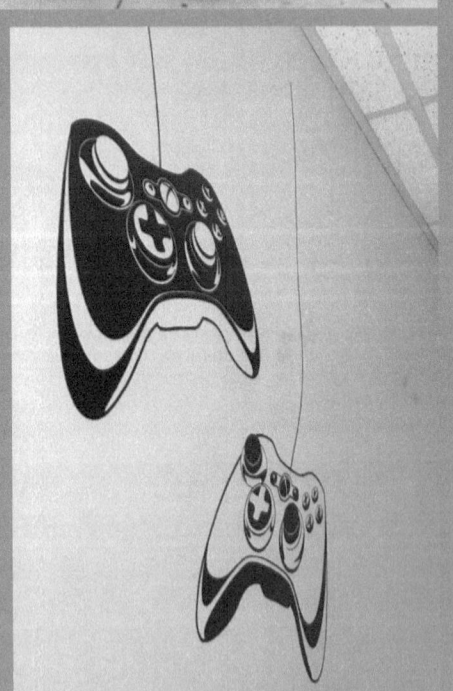

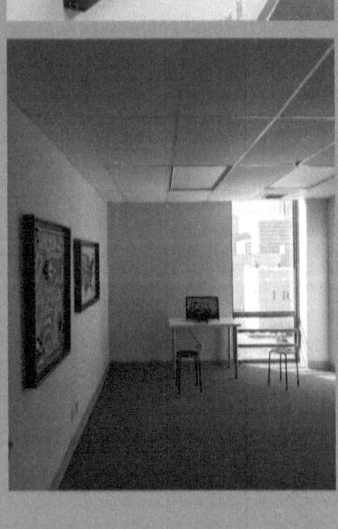

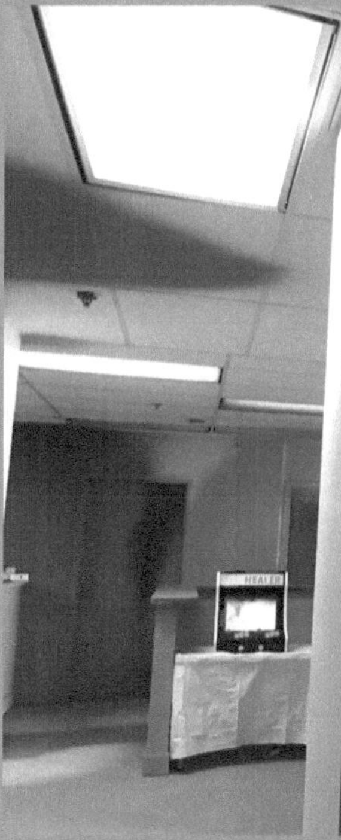

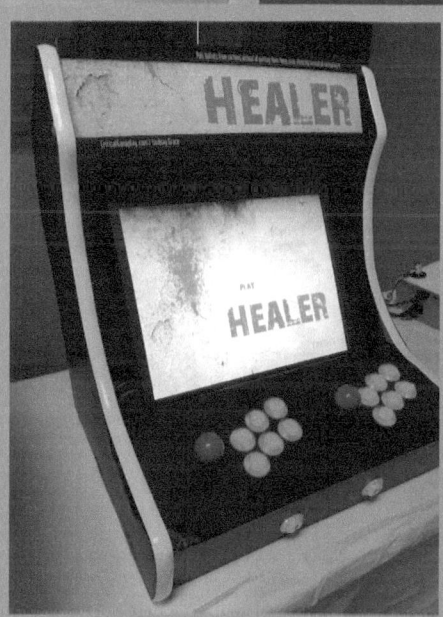

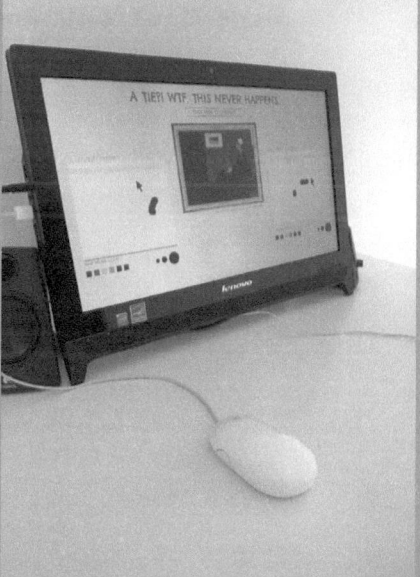

GRACE | TRAN | EWING

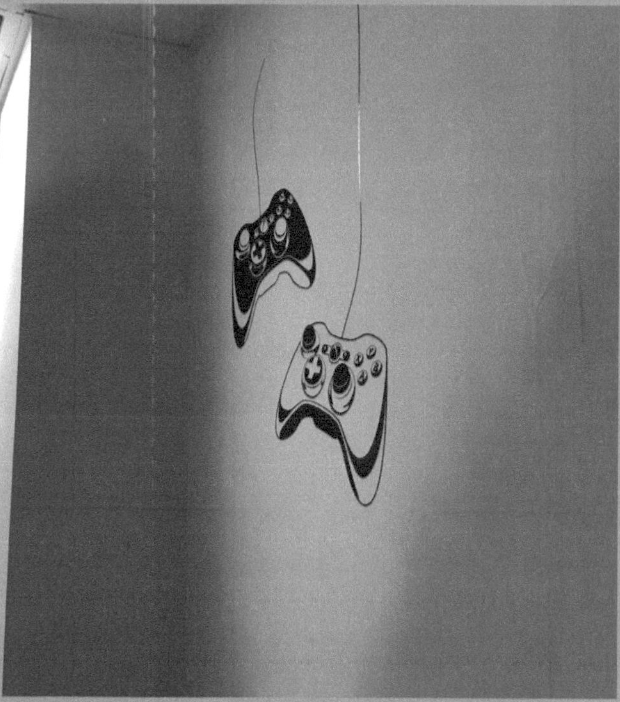

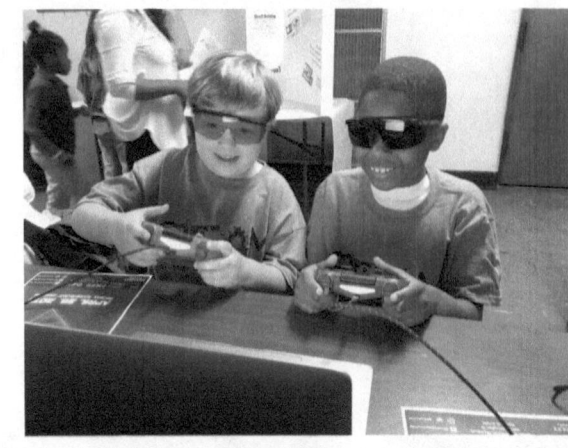

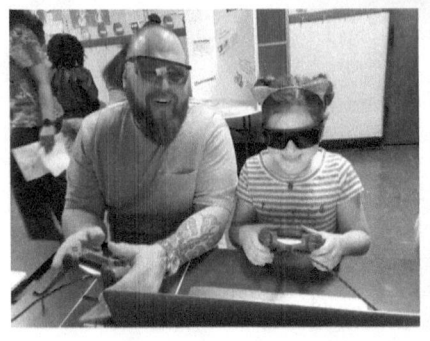

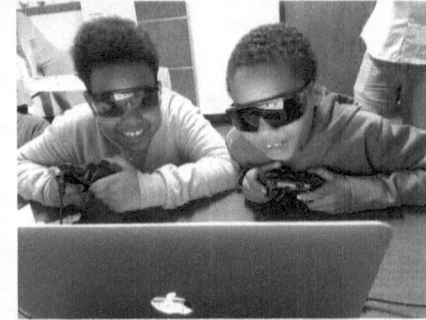

BVR

ETHAN HAM & SCOTT CAVANAH

BvR is a local, two-player competitive game. One player wears blue-tinted glasses and the other wears red-tinted glasses. The differing colors of the glasses allows for an experimental mechanic where certain objects can be visible to one player but not the other, even though both players are looking at the same game space on the same monitor.

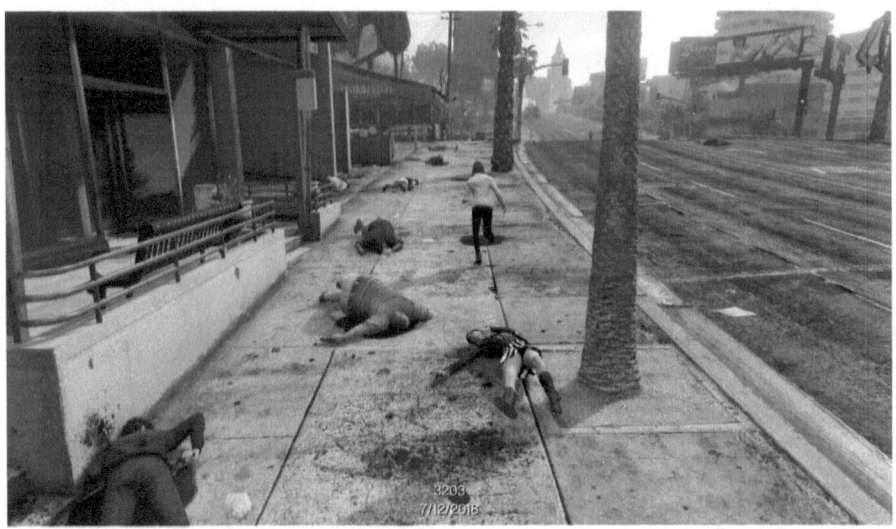

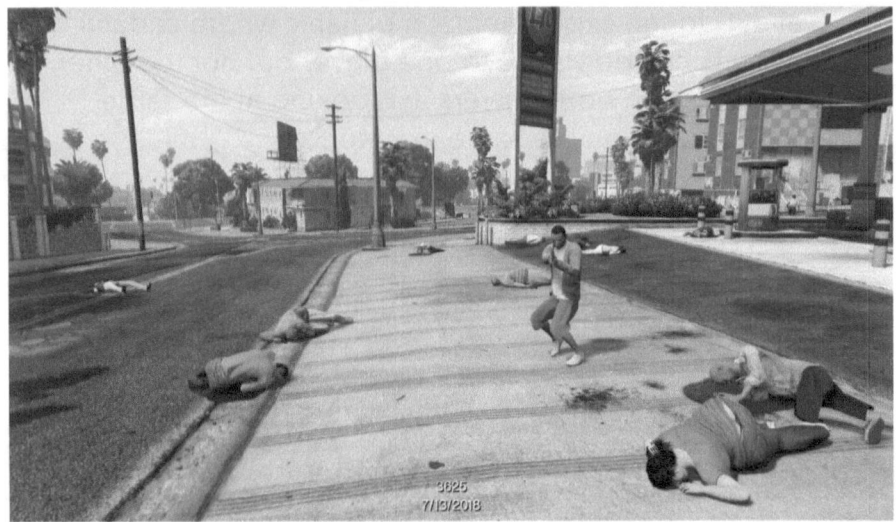

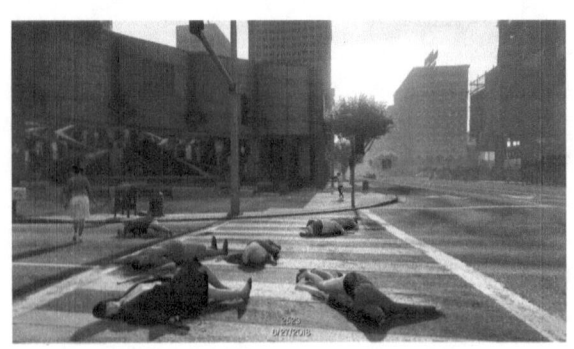

ELEGY: GTA USA GUN HOMICIDES

JOSEPH DeLAPPE

Elegy is a gaming mod for Grand Theft Auto V that reenacts each day of the total 2018 gun homicides since January 1st, 2018, as scraped from the Gun Violence Archive. Gun homicide totals since January 1st are revised daily on this website which are then fed directly into the project – starting at 0 each midnight Central time, each day the new total body count since January 1st is reenacted in its totality and so on. As of July 4th, 2018, there were 7,293 gun homicides in the United States – by the end of 2018 this number will likely reach close to 15,000. The project is being live screened on Twitch.tv.

The work is accompanied by a looping soundtrack, of the first radio recording of "God Bless America" as sung by Kate Smith in 1938. 2018 is the 100th anniversary of the composing of this song by Irving Berlin. The work is a pilot project to explore data visualization using computer gaming. The intention is to run the project 24/7 for the next year until July 4th, 2019.

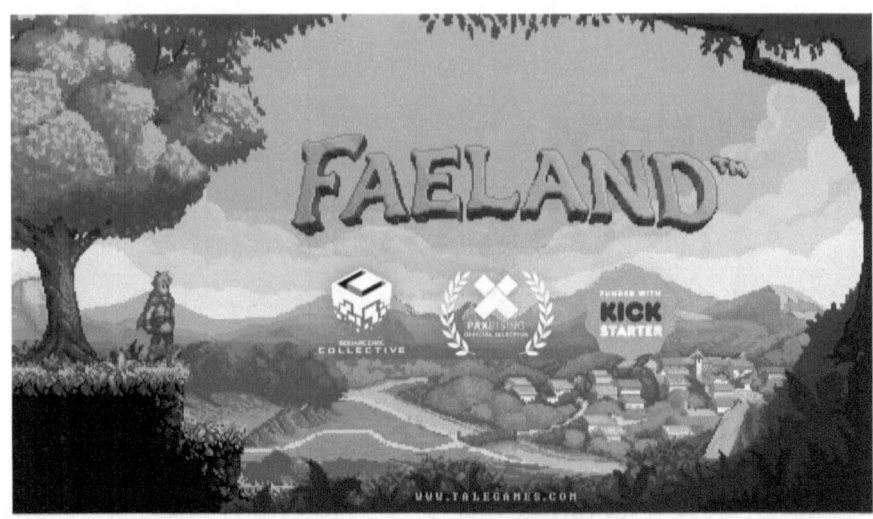

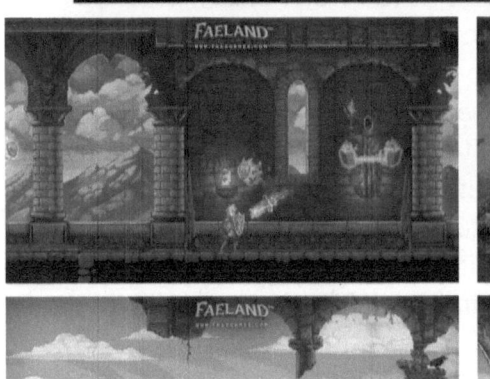

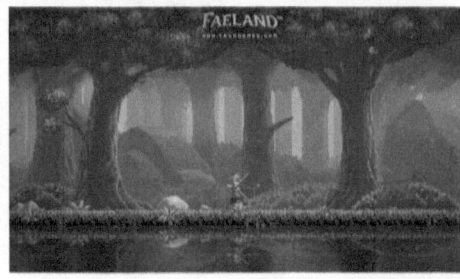

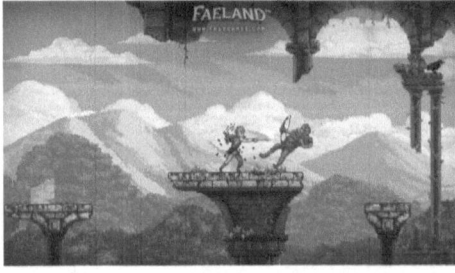

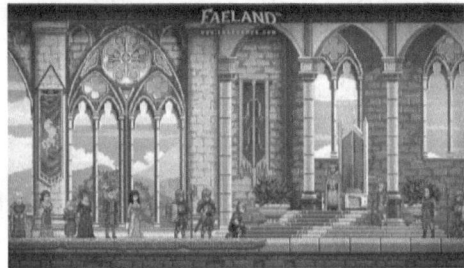

FAELAND

TALEGAMES LLC

Faeland is a 2D Platform Action Adventure Role Playing Indie Video Game set in a Medieval-Fantasy world currently in development for console and PC, inspired by the nostalgic 8-Bit classics. It offers modern charm for all generations.

FEATURES:

- Experience detailed handcrafted pixel-art graphic
- Engage in open world Metroidvania exploration style.
- Level up and learn new skills.
- Change your equipped weapons to match your preferred combat style.
- Enhance your armor and enjoy the look of new outfits on your character.
- Puzzles and riddles solving.
- Explore large dungeons with challenging boss battles.

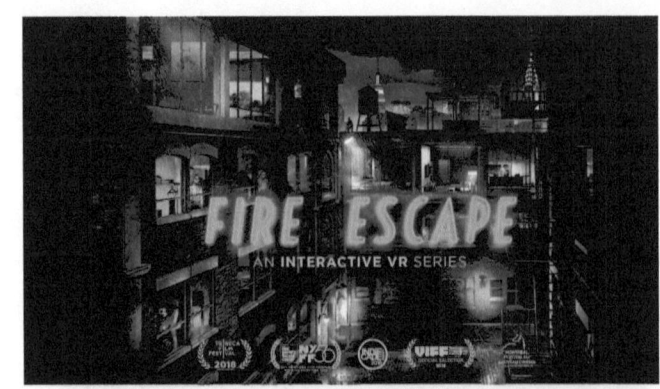

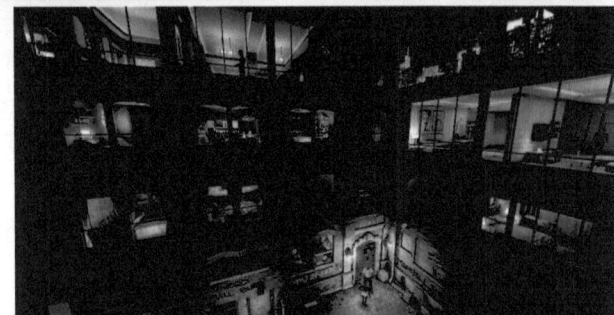

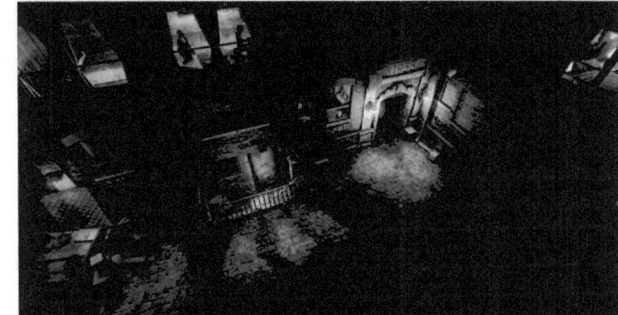

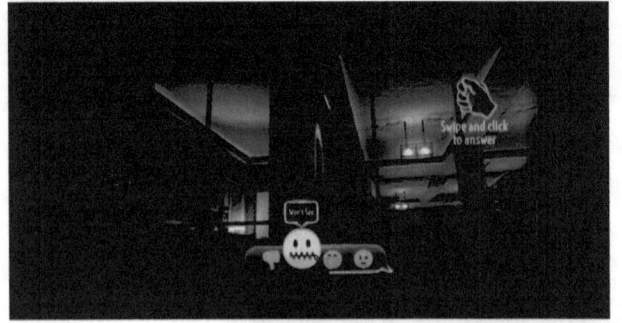

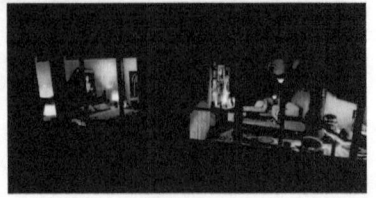

FIRE ESCAPE: AN INTERACTIVE VR SERIES

iNK STORIES

Through the fog of the city peer into the private lives of eight diverse New Yorkers from your fire escape to discover suspicion and deception—all unfolding in real time. Set against a shadowy backdrop of contemporary gentrification where disenfranchised tenants become twisted in a string of dark mysteries and a murder. Audiences exercise their voyeuristic tendencies in this rich and innovative interactive cinematic narrative which harnesses the strengths of virtual reality— where audiences must reconcile their own role as an observer to reveal the truth.

GRACE | TRAN | EWING

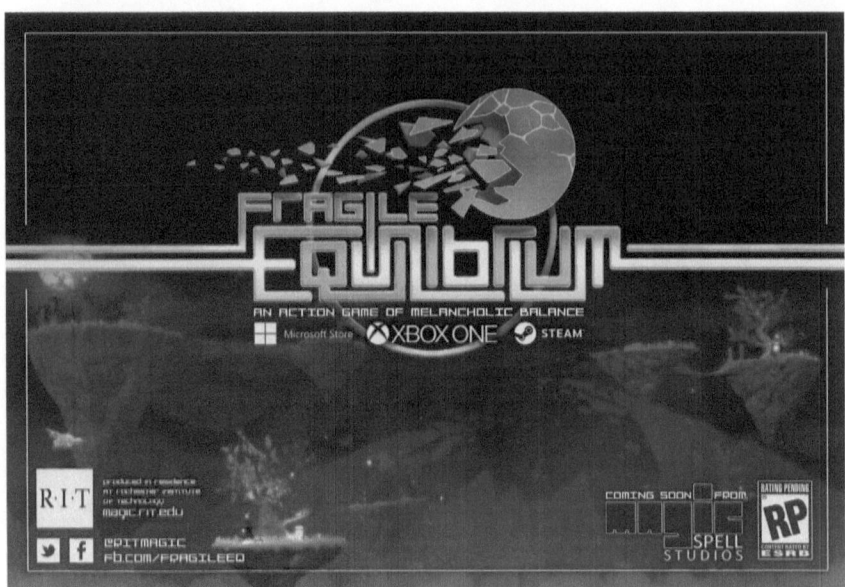

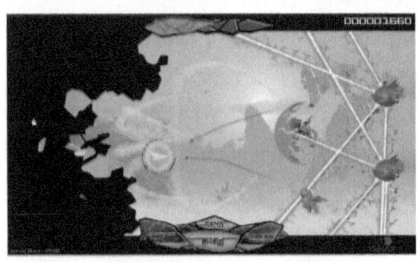

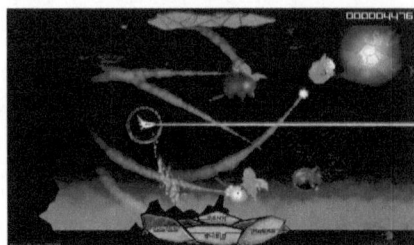

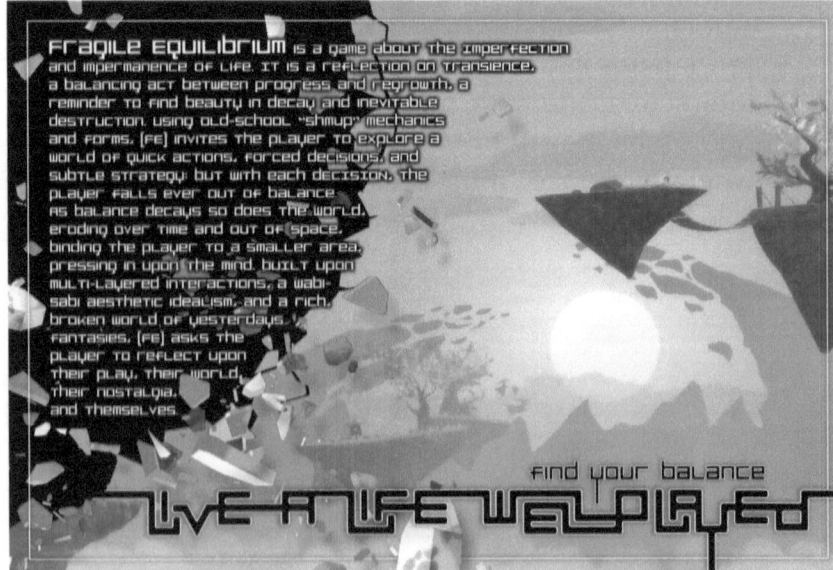

Fragile Equilibrium is a game about the imperfection and impermanence of life. It is a reflection on transience, a balancing act between progress and regrowth, a reminder to find beauty in decay and inevitable destruction. Using old-school "shmup" mechanics and forms, [FE] invites the player to explore a world of quick actions, forced decisions, and subtle strategy; but with each decision, the player falls ever out of balance. As balance decays so does the world, eroding over time and out of space, binding the player to a smaller area, pressing in upon the mind. Built upon multi-layered interactions, a wabi-sabi aesthetic idealism, and a rich, broken world of yesterday's fantasies, [FE] asks the player to reflect upon their play, their world, their nostalgia, and themselves.

find your balance

LIVE A LIFE WELL PLAYED

FRAGILE EQUILIBRIUM

MAGIC SPELL STUDIOS

Fragile Equilibrium (FE) is a game about the imperfection and impermanence of life. It is a reflection on transience, a balancing act between progress and regrowth, and a reminder to find beauty in decay and inevitable destruction. Using old-school "shmup" mechanics and forms, FE invites the player to explore a world of quick actions, forced decisions, and subtle strategy: but with each decision, it falls ever out of balance. As balance decays so does the world, eroding over time and out of space, binding the player to a smaller area, pressing in upon the mind. Built upon multi-layered interactions, a Wabi Sabi aesthetic idealism, and a rich, broken world of yesterday's fantasies, FE asks the player to reflect upon their play, their world, their nostalgia, and themselves. Find your balance, live a life well played.

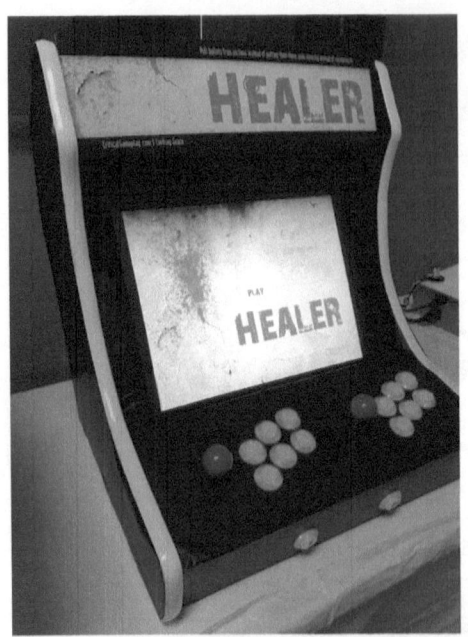

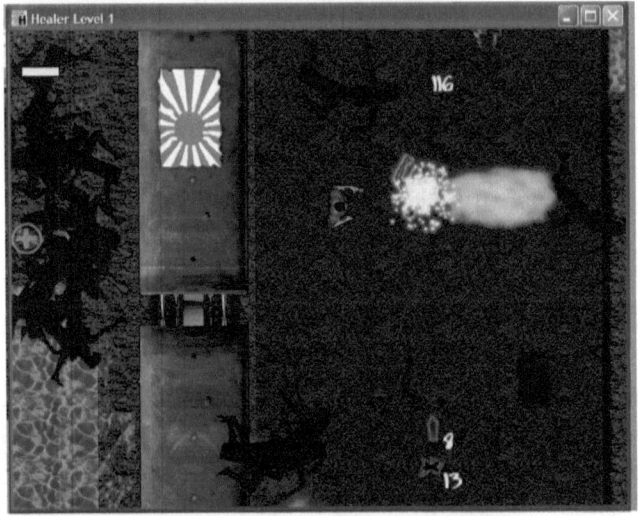

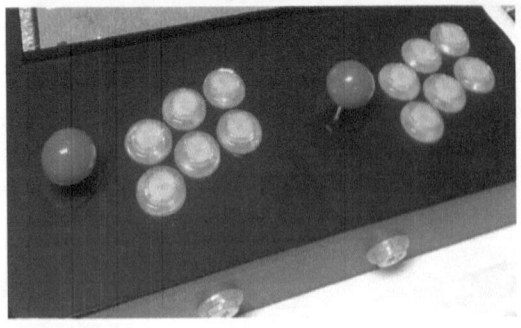

HEALER

CRITICAL GAMEPLAY

LINDSAY GRACE

Instead of shooting characters, players must heal victims of historical massacres. The player can reverse death, by pulling bullets from the victims. The soldiers that committed these massacres are still lurking, so the player must work to keep the recently revived alive. The player can put themselves between the bullet and the target or strategize to reverse the tragedy.

The game depicts the Nanking Massacre (1937-38), the largest historical atrocity whose fact and fiction were continuously debated.

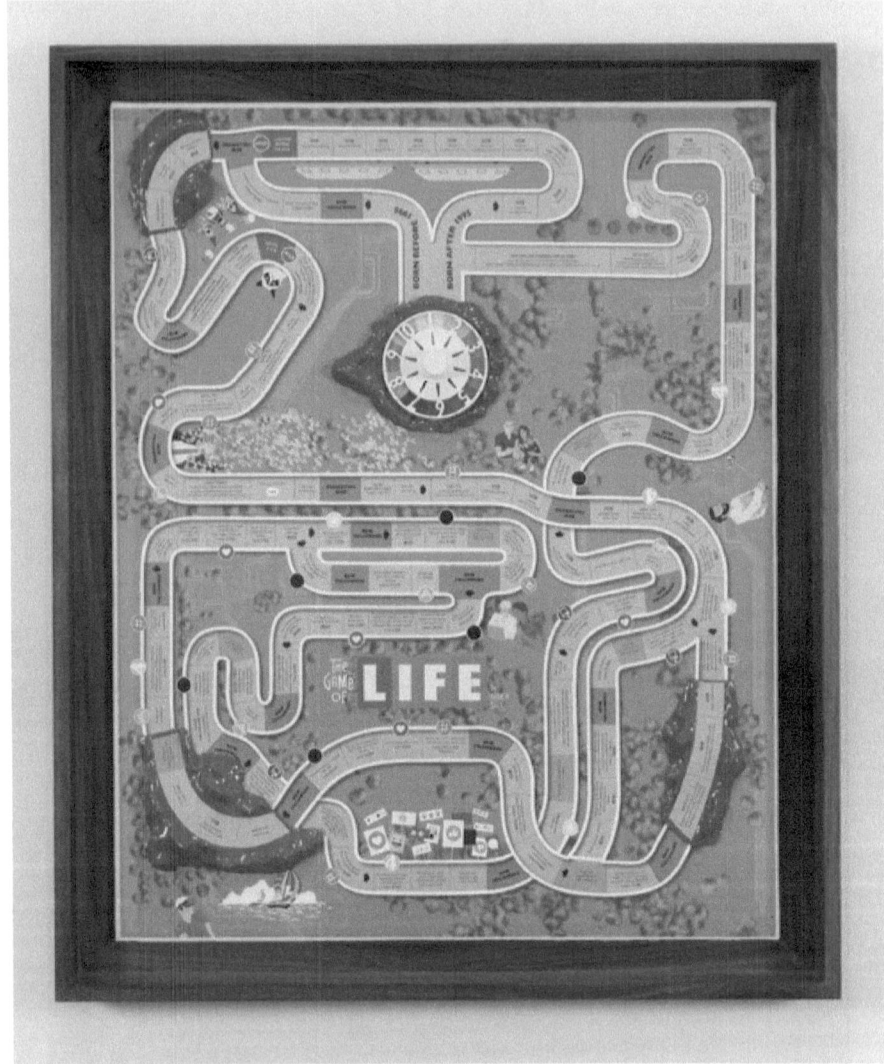

THE GAME OF LIFE: SOCIAL MEDIA EDITION

NANCY DALY

The Game of Life (Social Media Edition), based on the original Game of Life, asks players to move around the board collecting social media followers. Players are rewarded for actions that would get them followers in real life, like creating a popular meme and losing followers for not being internet savvy. Viewers will notice that when one gets to the end of the board - where one would retire in the original version - in this one, you must simply start over.

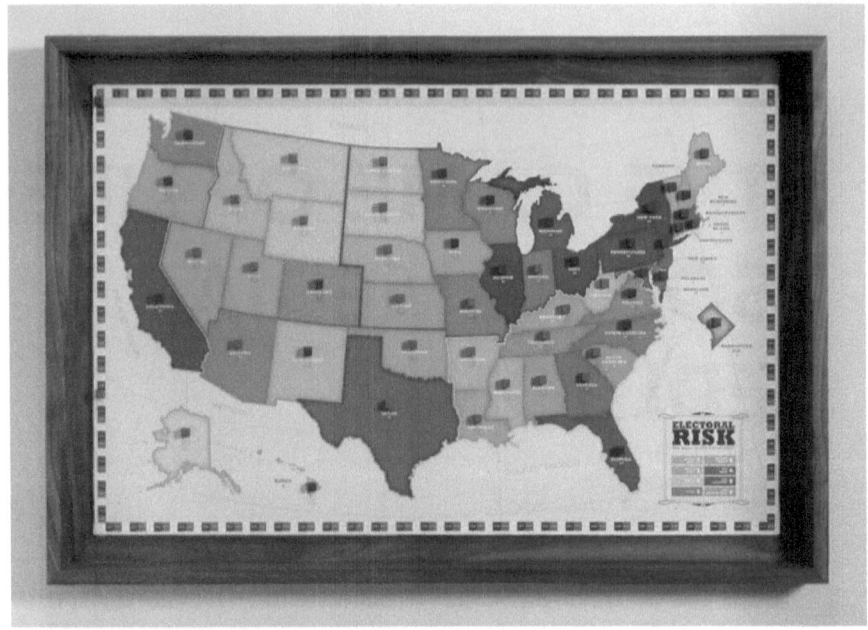

ELECTORAL RISK: THE GAME OF USA DOMINATION

NANCY DALY

Electoral Risk is an examination of our current electoral college process through the lens of the classic board game Risk. Through play, viewers will learn to develop common strategies employed by candidates to dominate the most strategic states in order to get to 270 electors. Electoral Risk equates current political campaign strategy with a war game.

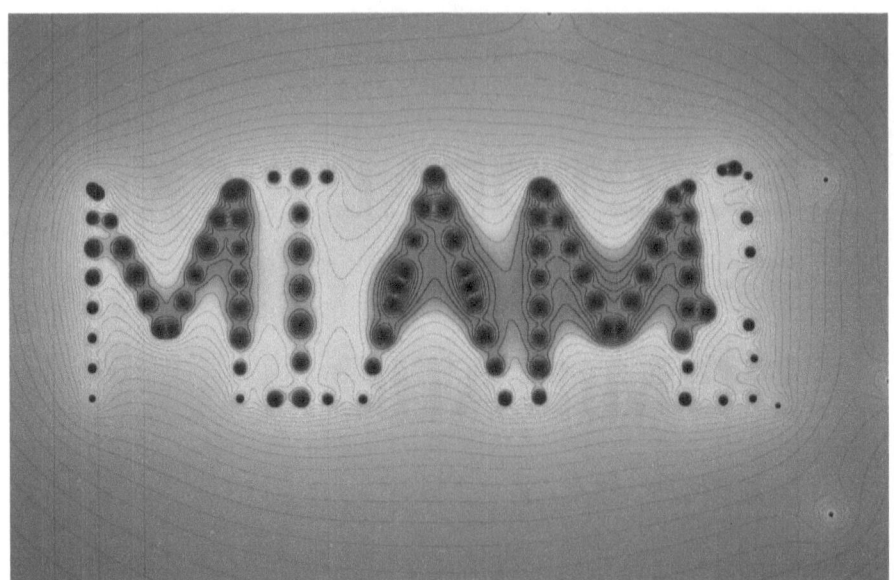

PARTICLE DISTANCE

NICK HARDEMAN

Particle Distance is an experiment visualizing the space between points of interest. Drawing inspiration from topographic maps, the area between the points are visualized with varying colors and lines depending on the distance. The points move and dance about the space or come together to form words.

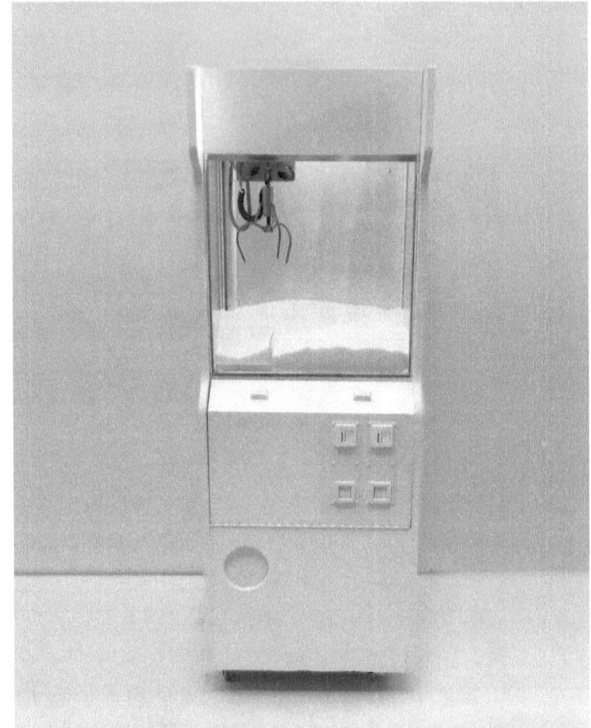

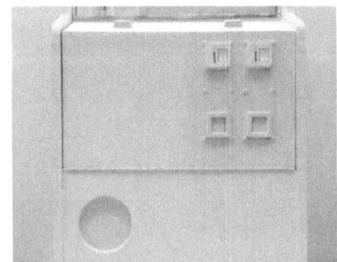

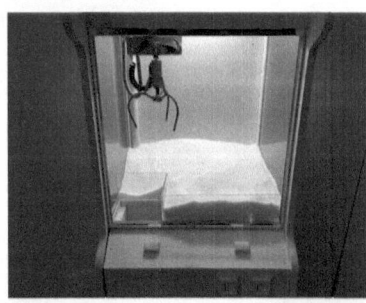

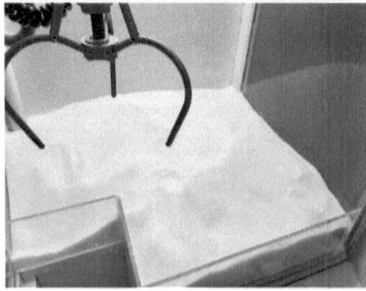

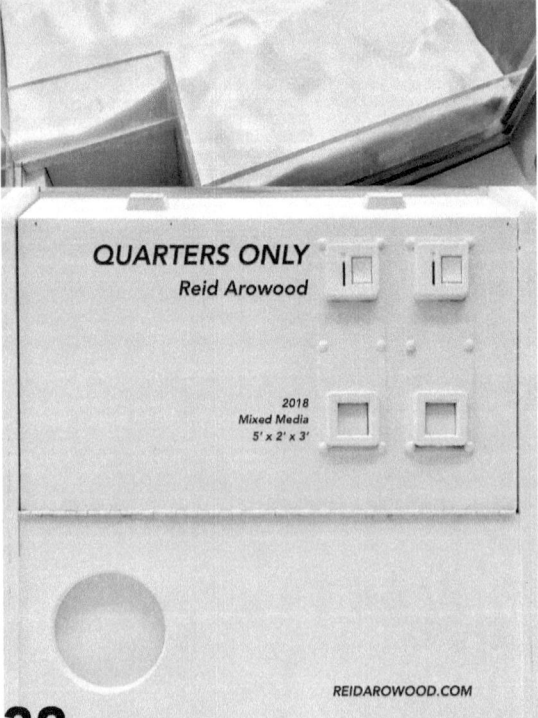

QUARTERS ONLY
Reid Arowood

2018
Mixed Media
5' x 2' x 3'

REIDAROWOOD.COM

QUARTERS ONLY

REID AROWOOD

Quarters Only is an arcade game with no direct goal or motivation other than curiosity. The player is faced with a completely neutral gaming platform with no instruction (other than the title itself, "Quarters Only"). By inserting a quarter, the game is activated. The player can operate two buttons to control a classic arcade claw. When the claw is lowered, it grabs at a pile of sand, leaving a slight footprint of the player's interaction. The player pays a quarter to explore, question, and decide for themselves what makes "Quarters Only" a game.

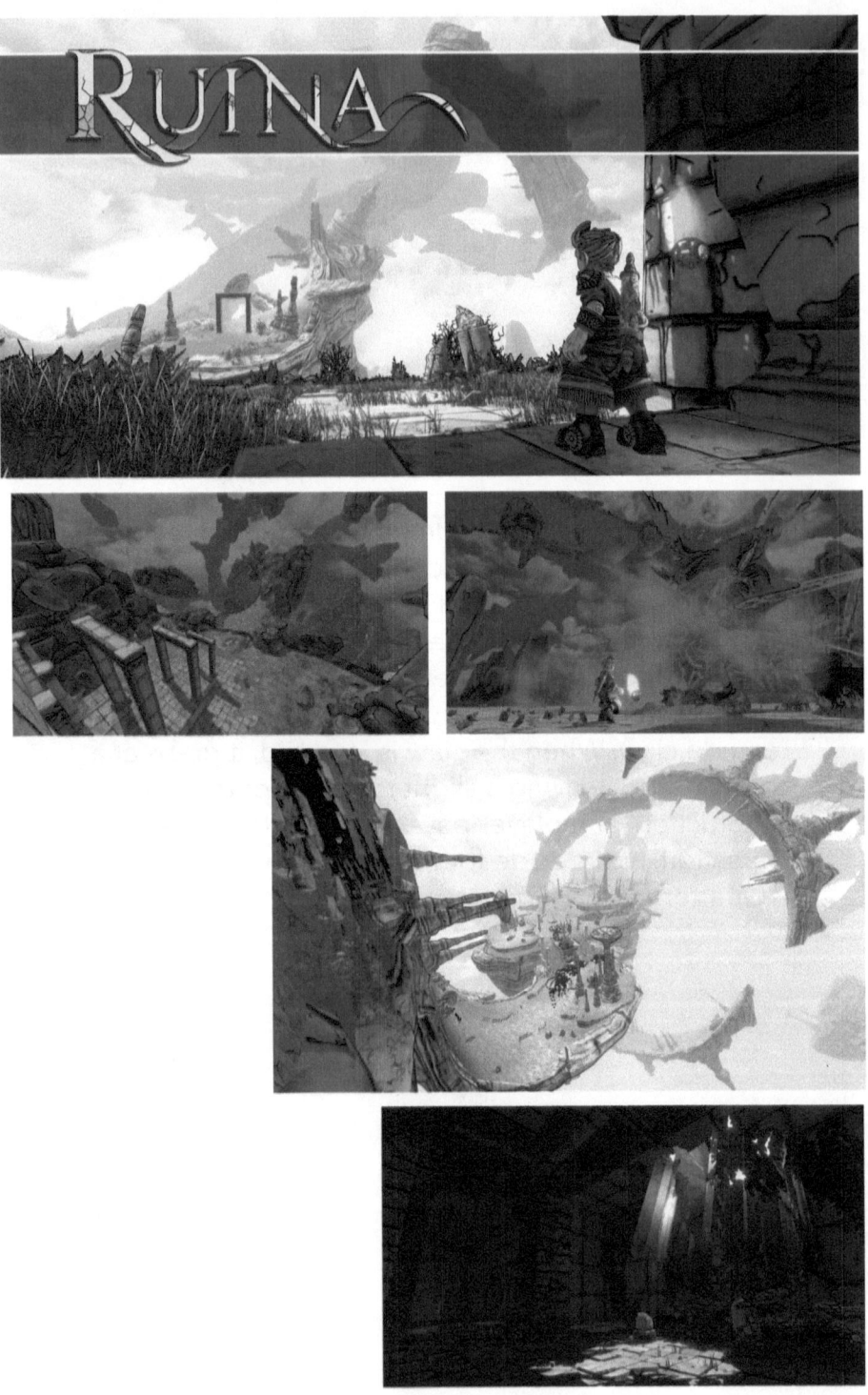

RUINA

JAKE NOLT & DAN NOLT

The game revolves around Evermore, an arrogant, self-centered adolescent forced to take a journey toward self-betterment. Pulled into the world of Eave, Evermore soon encounters a fire spirit named Ezra, who serves as a guide and conscience along the way. A great beast is responsible for Evermore's appearance in the twisting world, but these two are more intertwined than Evermore first understands. The game served as a cathartic examining of our personal faults and beliefs. The world's logic and lore developed as we dug deeper, finding things about ourselves that we had not anticipated on encountering.

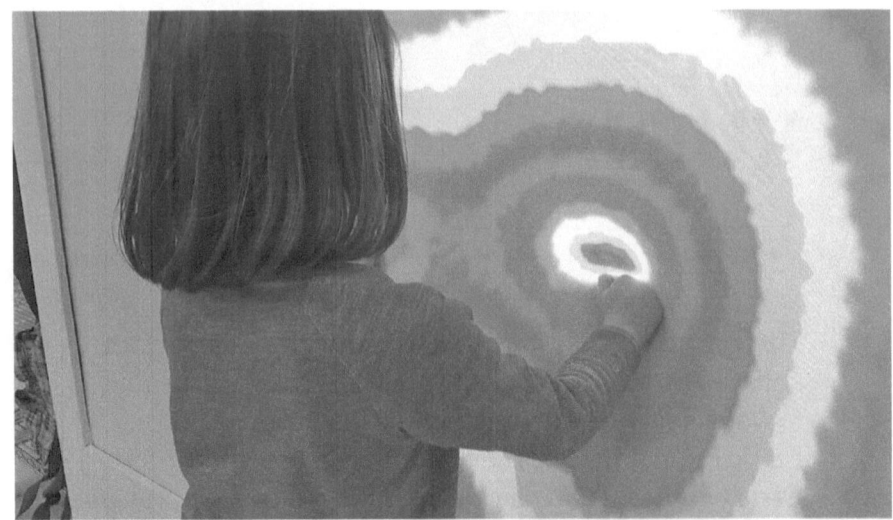

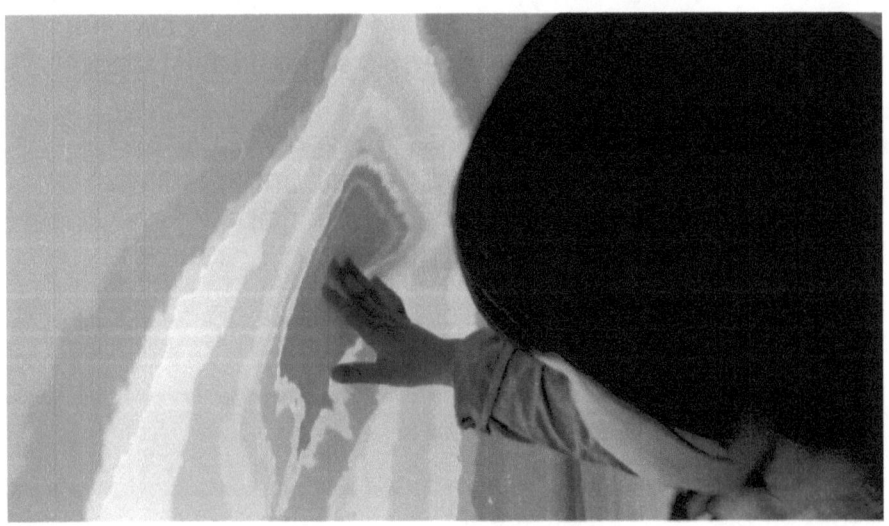

SENSORY IMAGING

ADRIAN SAS

A "magic" screen displays brilliant bursts of color wherever it is touched and impressed. The deeper or firmer the touch, the bigger the burst of color! Radiating color from the point of contact and rendering a four-dimensional map of one's movements, the installation's interface creates a mindful connection between sight, touch and movement which promotes somatosensory processing, develops cognition, and can build confidence in children. Most of all, it's just plain fun!

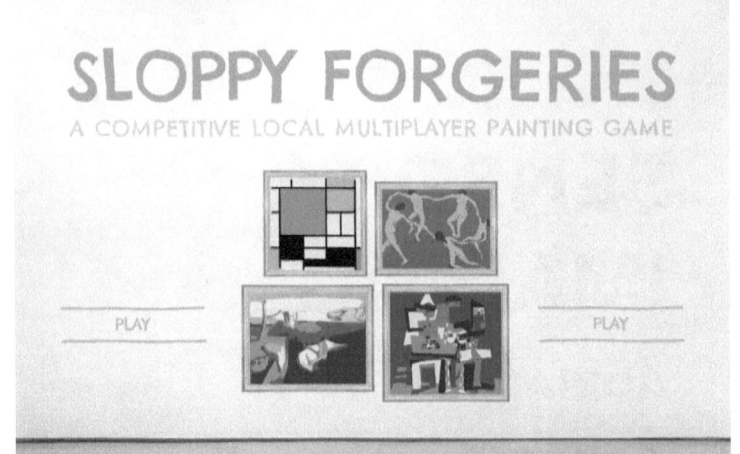

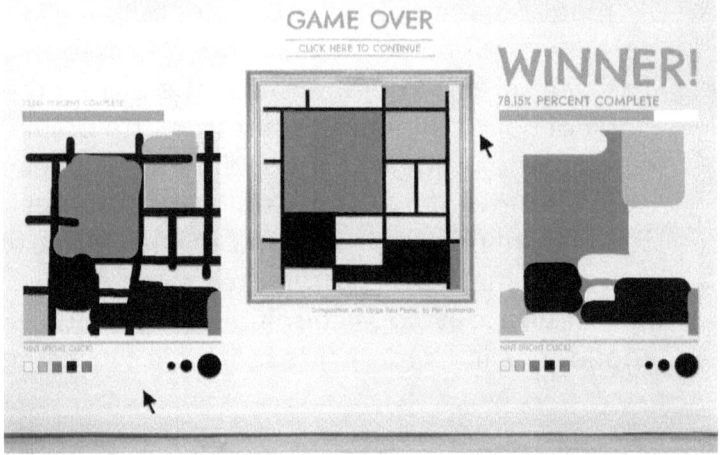

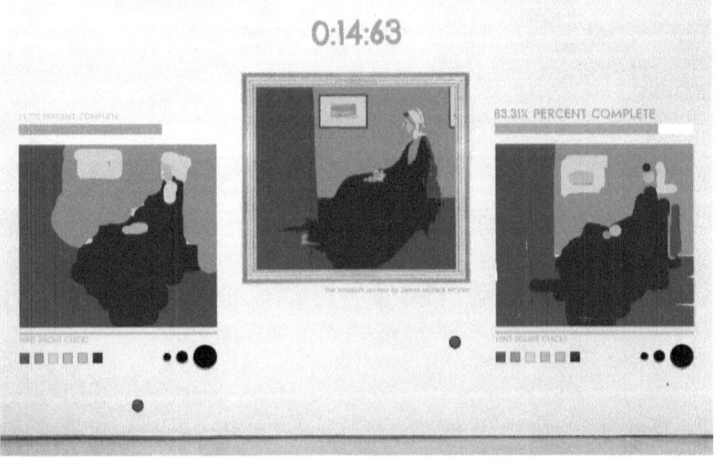

SLOPPY FORGERIES

JONAH WARREN

Sloppy Forgeries is a fast-paced, two-player local multiplayer painting game. Each player is given a mouse, a blank canvas, and a few simple paint tools. Each round, a famous painting from art history is revealed. Players race to copy the painting as quickly and accurately as possible.

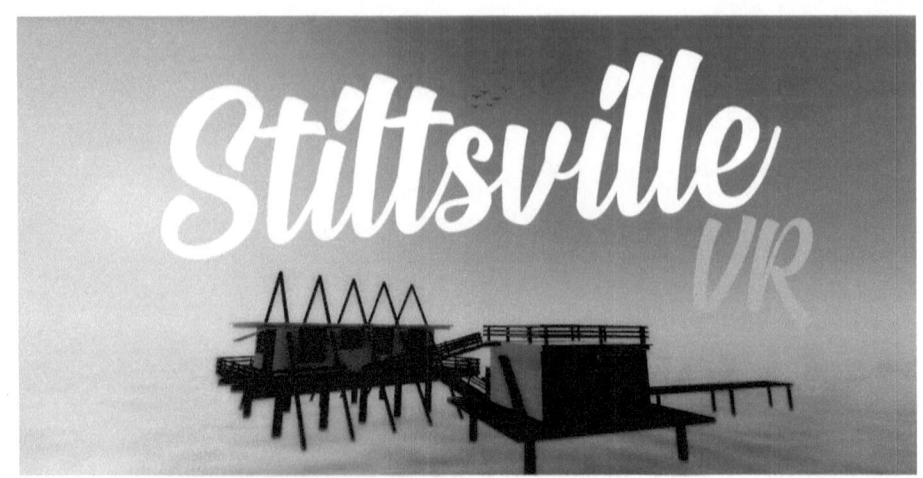

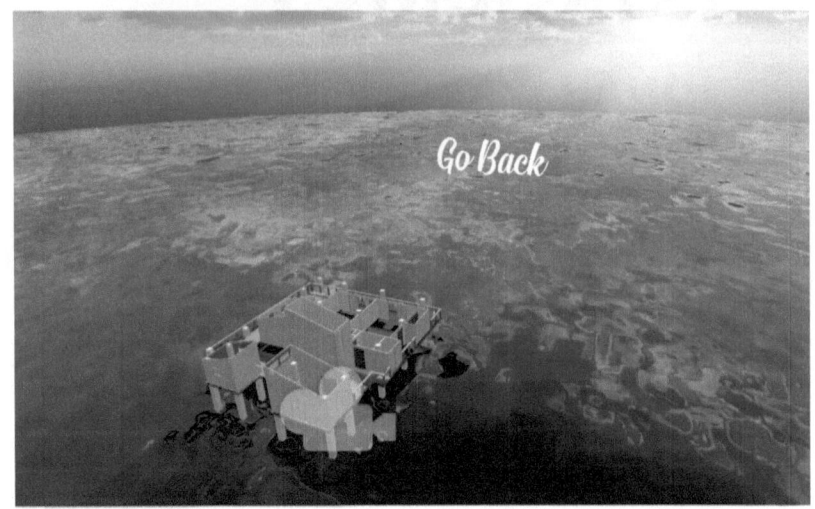

STILTSVILLE VR

NERDLAB WITH FILMGATE

Stiltsville VR allows global visitors and locals alike to explore Miami's iconic Stiltsville, the seven homes on stilts off the coast of Miami in Biscayne Bay, with an interactive virtual reality (VR) experience. This experience allows access to these iconic and hard-to-reach houses on a much larger scale than is currently possible. We cannot bring the world to Stiltsville, but we can bring Stiltsville to the world.

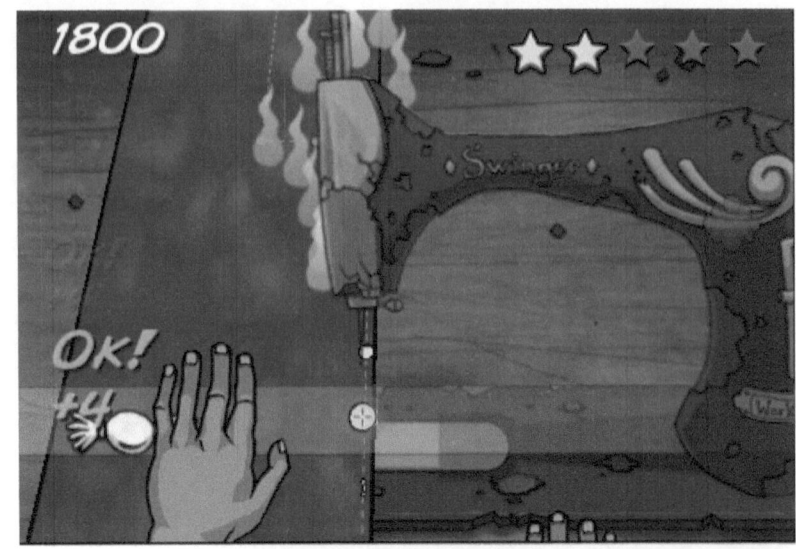

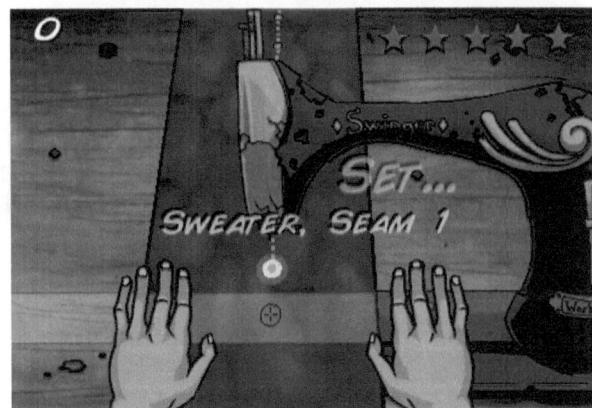

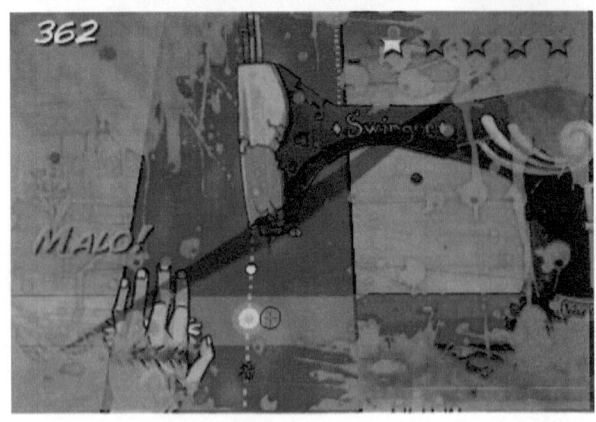

SWEATSHOP SUPERSTAR

CLAY EWING & LAWRENCE MASCIA

A bloody rhythm action game that explores the physical and emotional disposition of tedious sweatshop work through game mechanics.

In the game you play as Pepe, an 8-year-old boy forced into labor. "Sewing" through various garments, you plot your escape. Tilt controls guide your fingers as you stitch together fabric on an erratic sewing machine. Expertise and efficiency are rewarded through increasingly faster gameplay. Failure meets the crack of a whip.

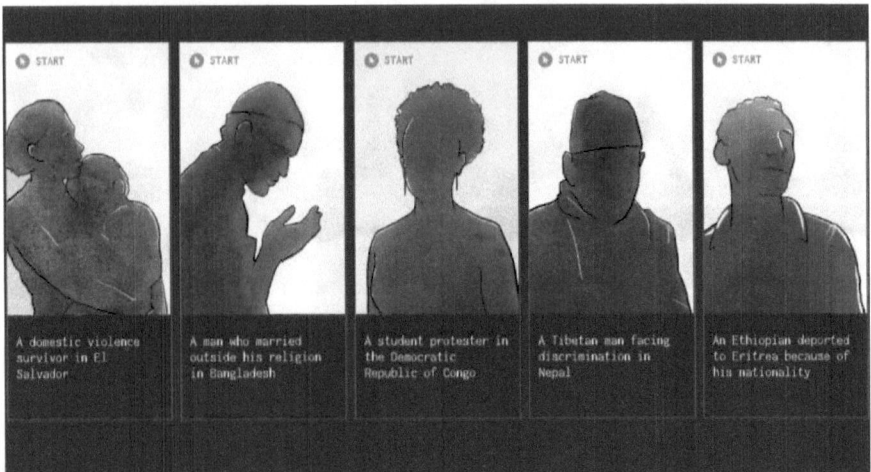

THE WAITING GAME

PLAYMATIC with PRO PUBLICA

The Waiting Game gives players the experience of what it is like to seek asylum in the United States. The game features five anonymized real stories of people from different parts of the world who sought entry into the US. The game is designed to be a piece of journalism that supplements a long-form written piece from Pro Publica and a radio piece from WNYC. The Waiting Game works by embodying the experience of the asylum seeker and asks the user how long they would wait to reach the end of their journey.

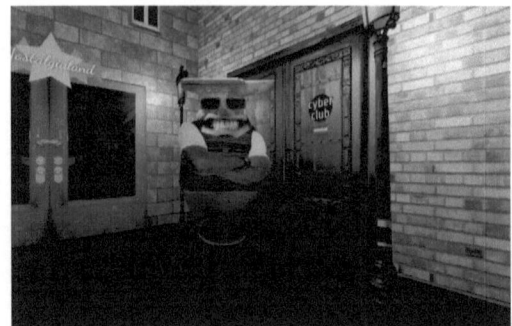

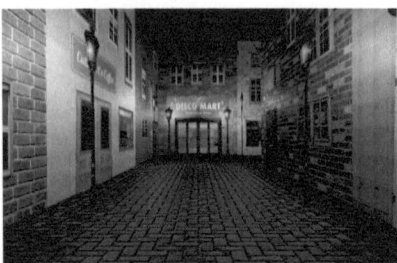

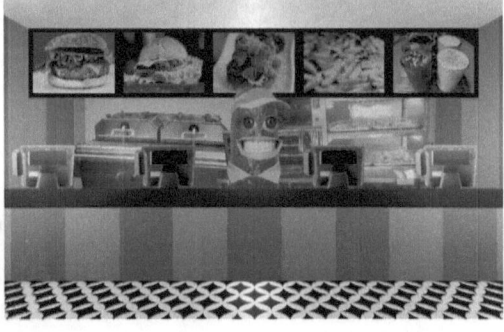

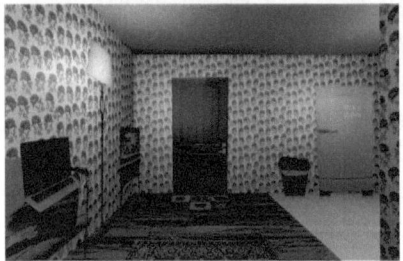

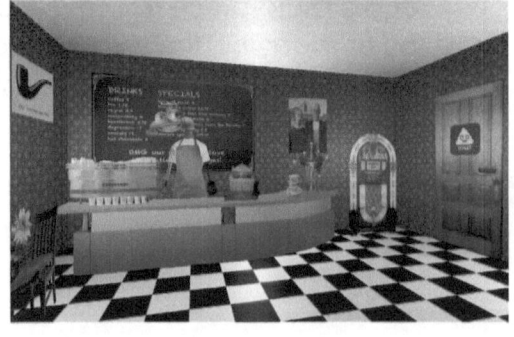

YOU USED TO BE SOMEONE

DIETRICH SQUINKIFER

You have no idea how long it's been since you last set foot outside your cramped little apartment. You don't really talk to anyone. You can't focus on work. You barely have any appetite to speak of, literally and figuratively. Even casually reading Twitter makes you anxious.

Somehow, you thought moving to a new city would help you meet people you actually like and that you'd find fun activities to do and better opportunities all around. You used to be pretty good at faking your way around being a social butterfly. People actually seemed to like you, and the stuff you made and performed. But now? You can't even remember being that person.

Maybe you should go outside.
Maybe it will help.

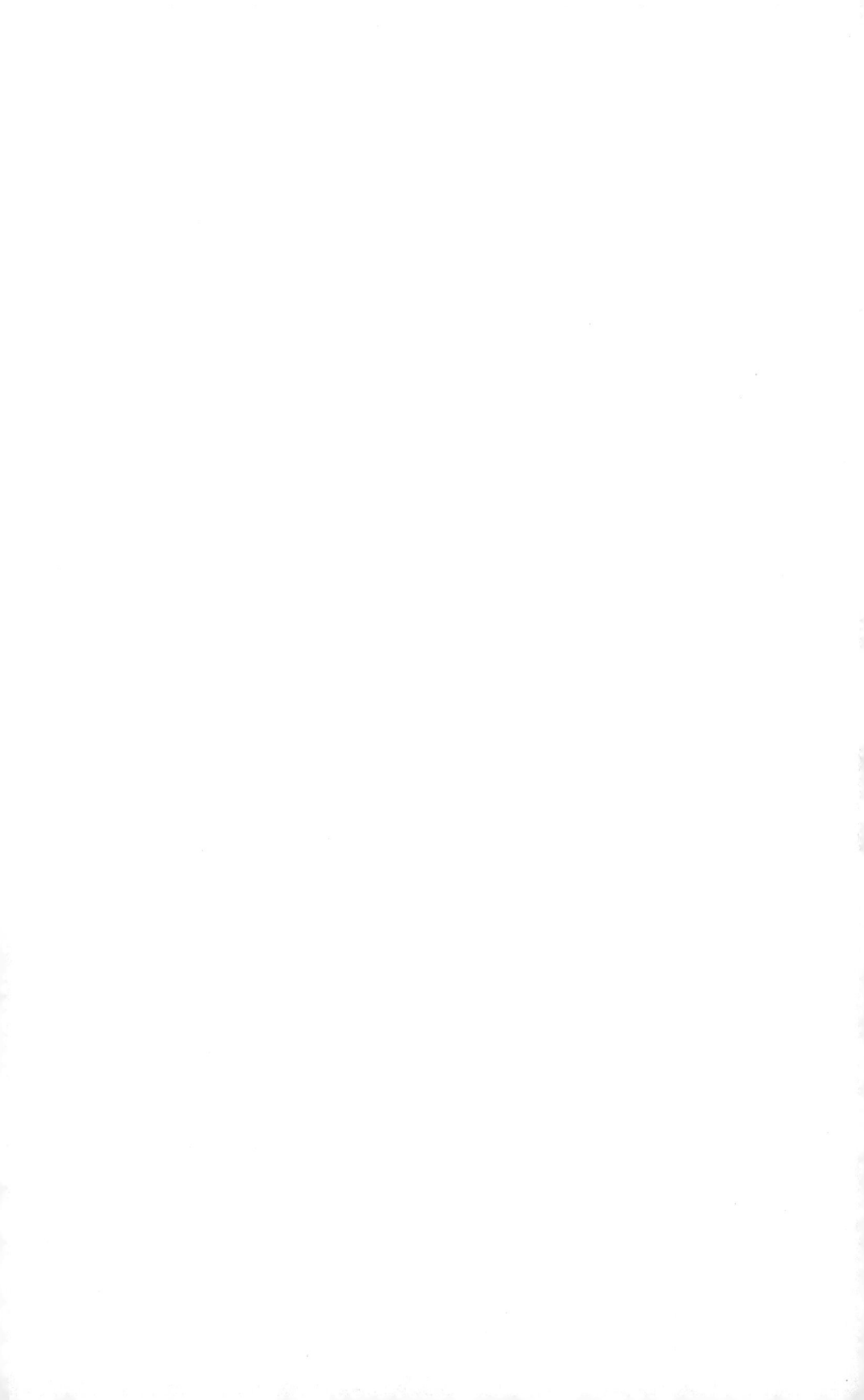

www.ingramcontent.com/pod-product-compliance
Lightning Source LLC
Chambersburg PA
CBHW021048180526
45163CB00005B/2333